# You, me, and the

# SUPER

# LOVE

By
Claire Murphy

Illustrated by
Claudia Gadotti

**You, Me, and the Superlove** by Claire Murphy

Illustrations by Claudia Gadotti

This is a work of fiction. Names, characters, places and incidents are either products of the author's imagination or are used fictitiously, and any resemblance to any persons, living or dead, business establishments, events or locales is entirely coincidental.

First Edition: Feb 2014

ISBN-10: 1505297273

ISBN-13: 978-1505297270

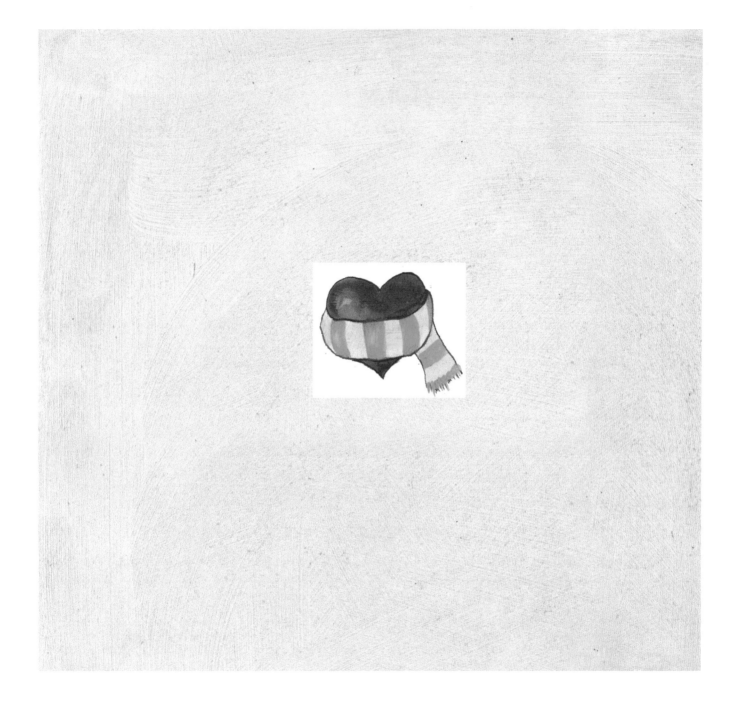

This Superlove Book
belongs to

_____

Holly was zooming around the kitchen on her scooter. Holly knew she shouldn't do that in the house, but it was raining outside and it was
*Fun!*
*Fun!*
*Fun!*

Mummy was putting away some
cups and plates from the dishwasher.

Holly stopped on her scooter. She had
a big question that she wanted to ask Mummy

'Mummy, why does Daddy not live here at home with us?'

Mummy put down the cloth she had been using to wipe some plates.

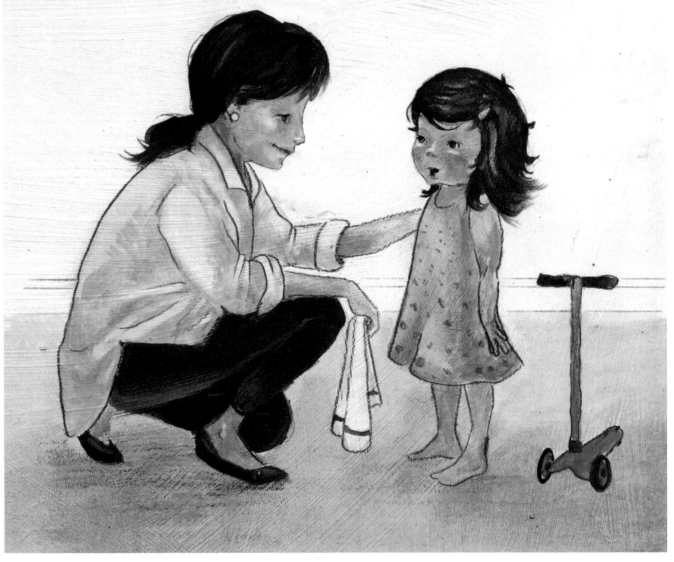

'Let me come back to the dishes later.

I can finish the jobs after we have had a little chat.

I am going to tell you all about **The Superlove**!'


'About what Mummy?' asked Holly.

Snuggle into this armchair with me and I will explain.
Holly squished into the giant armchair next to her mummy.

'Daddy doesn't live with us right now. I won't tell you all the details because
a lot of it is grown-up peoples' stuff.

There are some very very important things you should know Holly

None of this is your fault. Mummy and Daddy know that you are just wonderful!'

'But why isn't daddy here?' Holly asked mummy.

'Because he has got some things that he needs to
figure out and learn about himself"
Sometimes thinking about these things can take a lot of time.

It's like when you get a new jigsaw puzzle, it takes you
some time to figure out how the pieces fit together.

I don't know when daddy may be around again.

So right now it's just

You, me and the **Superlove!**'

'What's the Superlove Mummy?

Holly asked.

'Well Holly, while your daddy is away he gave me some of his love powers just for you.
That means that I can give you
the mummy love, and some of the daddy love,
which makes ….

'But how do I see the Superlove Mummy?'

'Oh you don't see the Superlove darling,

..... but you do feel it.

You can feel the Superlove wrap around you when you put on your coat on a very cold day.

You can feel the Superlove when you open your lunchbox at school and there is a surprise note inside.

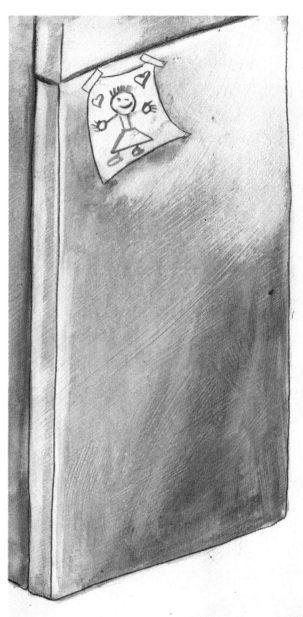

You can feel the Superlove when you come home and the picture that you drew is hanging on our fridge.

You can feel the Superlove when
you are in your bath surrounded by your bubbles and favorite toys.

You can feel the Superlove just before you close your eyes

and when you snuggle down in your bed every single night.'

'So right now Mummy, it's just you me and the Superlove?' Holly said.

'Yes darling. The Superlove from mummy and daddy is always with you, no matter where you are, or where mummy and daddy are,' mummy said.

'Remember Holly, you can ask me questions about this anytime.

Now, up you get! I think you need to help me finish emptying the dishwasher!!

Holly walked back into the kitchen with mummy.

It was good to know that the Superlove from mummy and daddy was always around.

She was glad they'd had their chat.

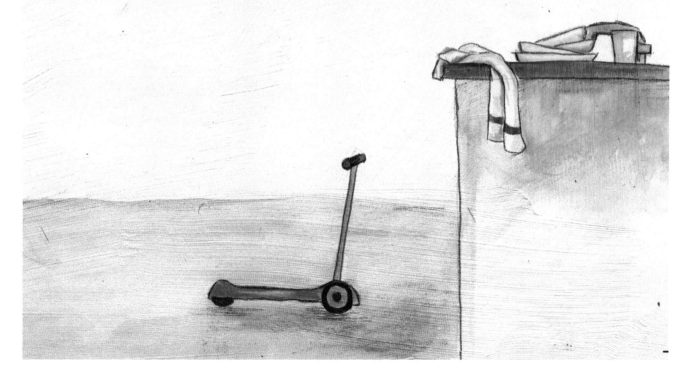

Holly could already feel
the Superlove
all around

Printed in Great Britain
by Amazon